"I like to write about me, because I know about me."

John Lennon

JOHN'S SEC D

RET REAMS

The Life of John Lennon

written by
Doreen Rappaport

illustrated by
Bryan Collier

Hyperion Books for Children ✿ New York

For Bob,
in celebration of our sixties
—D.R.

To Mrs. Cushner and the
children of the Browning School
—B.C.

The author thanks the students of Mike Alberci's music classes at Maple Street School in Hopkinton, New Hampshire, for their insightful critiques of her manuscript. The author and illustrator wish to thank Maureen Sullivan, Garen Thomas, and Anne Diebel, who helped John's dreams come alive. Special thanks to Yoko Ono.

AUTHOR'S NOTE

Forty years ago, on a Sunday night in February 1964, an English rock 'n' roll group called the Beatles appeared on American television for the first time. I was one of 73 million Americans who watched John Lennon, Paul McCartney, George Harrison, and Ringo Starr perform. Instantly, I was "wild" about them. For the next ten years I bought every new Beatles album. (In those days, we had "records," not CDs.) In the beginning, John Lennon and Paul McCartney wrote all the songs. Lennon and McCartney put both their names on every song, even if one had written it alone. The Beatles' music grew more complex in the ten years they played together. When the group split up, each man took a different musical path and was individually praised.

This book is about John Lennon, one of the greatest figures in the history of popular music. To write this book, I read biographies of him, hundreds of transcribed radio, television, and print interviews; and autobiographical pieces; and, of course, I listened over and over to his music. I call my book *John's Secret Dreams*, because in his writings, John speaks of the impact those dreams had on every element of his life. I share some of them with you, along with some of his songs, which touched the hearts of people all over the world.

—Doreen Rappaport

ILLUSTRATOR'S NOTE

Creating the art for this book has been the greatest challenge of my career. I didn't grow up listening to John Lennon or the Beatles. They were foreign to me and yet so familiar to everyone else. I had to get past the pressure to live up to the experiences of others and, instead, concentrate on the ones I would soon have myself.

John Lennon's life inspired me to create my art in a painterly way I never had used before. It forced me to consider structure, anatomy, and organic movement—the wind around a figure—to illustrate thoughts and dreams. I had to figure out how to tell a story that was fresh to me but didn't necessarily follow the text, and instead alluded to it.

In order to get into John's world, I listened to his music and conversations. I read into what he was saying and *not* saying. I heard the blues in his songs. When I learned that John had lost his own perspective, when his feelings of emptiness and soul searching came into play, I found a connection. The first things that popped into my head were circles: circles of various meanings and functions. Circles are both chaotic and centering at the same time: life circles, record albums, confusing traps, piercing eyes, halos of light, or flashes of inspiration.

At the end of the day, I believe a dream of John's is that, when we walk outside and look at the stars in wonder, those stars are looking back at us in wonder.

—Bryan Collier

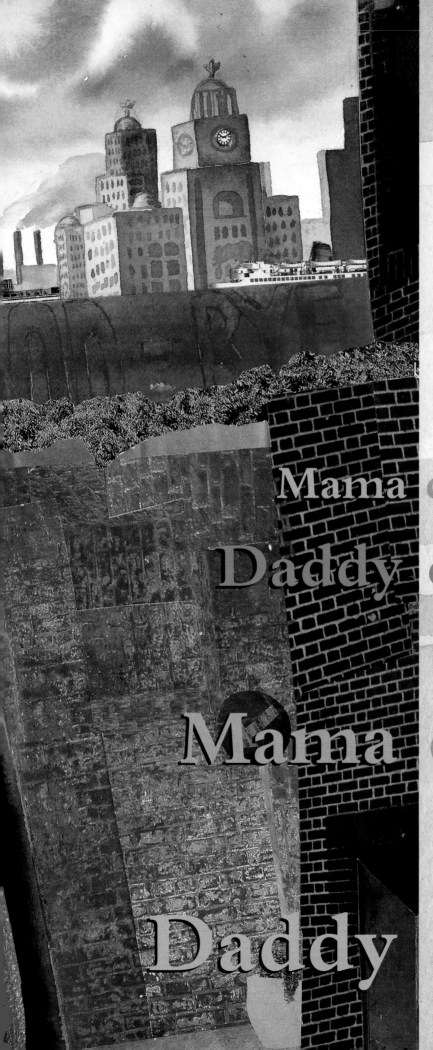

John's mother took his hand.
They left their house
in the Penny Lane district
of Liverpool, England,
to go to his new home
with Aunt Mimi and Uncle George.

His father, a merchant marine,
was away at sea.
His mother, feeling trapped,
didn't want to take care of him.
John was only five years old.

Mama don't go,

Daddy come home.

Mama don't go,

Daddy come home.

"Hey, you've got to

Aunt Mimi was caring but strict.
No roughhousing.
No comics.
But her house was filled with books.

Uncle George taught John how to read.
John loved Lewis Carroll and
his funny-sounding rhymes.
'Twas brillig, and the slithy toves
Did gyre and gimble in the wabe . . .

John wrote his own stories
and drew pictures to go with them.
How wonderful to be
a poet or an artist.
But Aunt Mimi would never allow it.
So John kept his dream a secret.

Ev'rywhere people stare each and ev'ry day.

I can see them laugh at me And I hear them say:

hide your love away!"

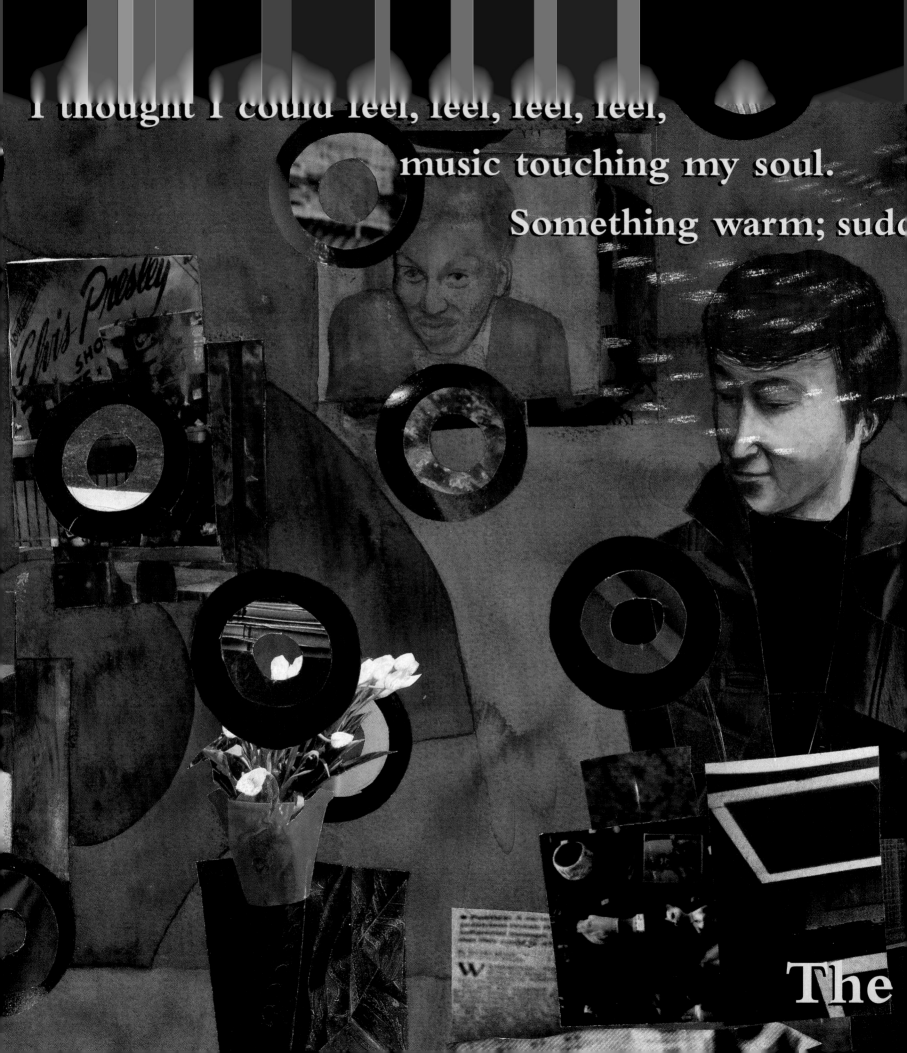

I thought I could feel, feel, feel, feel,
music touching my soul.
Something warm; sud

The

n cold.

pirit dance

When John was sixteen,
his mother came back into his life.
A musical craze called "skiffle"
was sweeping Liverpool then.
John wanted a guitar.
Aunt Mimi said no.
His mother bought him a banjo.
John formed his own band.

Sailors brought back records from America.
Little Richard, rattling the piano,
whooping, hooting, and howling.
Chuck Berry, poet of rock,
singing upward slides.
And Elvis Presley, the King.
Wailing, groaning, growling,
singing of heartbreak and loneliness.
Feelings John had, but was too afraid to share.

Rock 'n' roll—

grabbing John's heart,
a driving beat shaking his being.
A revolution of rhythm and sound.
It changed the world.
It changed John Lennon.

John
John
John was unfolding

I mean

as just seventeen

At a gig John met Paul McCartney,
who could play guitar upside down,
while John knew only two chords.
John asked him to join the group,
and they started writing songs.

They made up a melody
and sang it over and over
until they knew it by heart.

They worked on the lyrics.
John wrote one line.
Paul wrote another.

Not long after, John's mother died.
It hurt too much to cry.

Mother, you had me
but I never had you

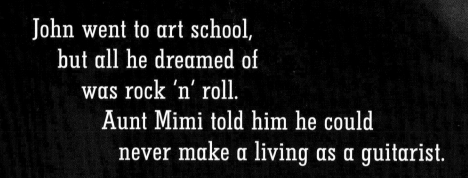

John went to art school,
but all he dreamed of
was rock 'n' roll.
Aunt Mimi told him he could
never make a living as a guitarist.

George Harrison, who
played guitar better
than either John or Paul,
joined the group.
They played in
smoky nightclubs,
dressed in black leather
and Texas cowboy boots.

Throw the mike around.
Lie down on the floor.
Shout. Jump. Stomp. Sing.

My heart went boom
when I crossed that room

The Beatles recorded John and Paul's songs
with a new drummer, Ringo Starr.

Well, she looked at me,
and I, I could see
That before too long
I'd fall in love with her.

Love, love me do,
you know I love you

W H A M !
One hit single after another,
One, two, three gold albums.
Top of the charts,
Top of the world,
and only twenty-four years old.

Yeah,
yeah,
yeah,
yeah!

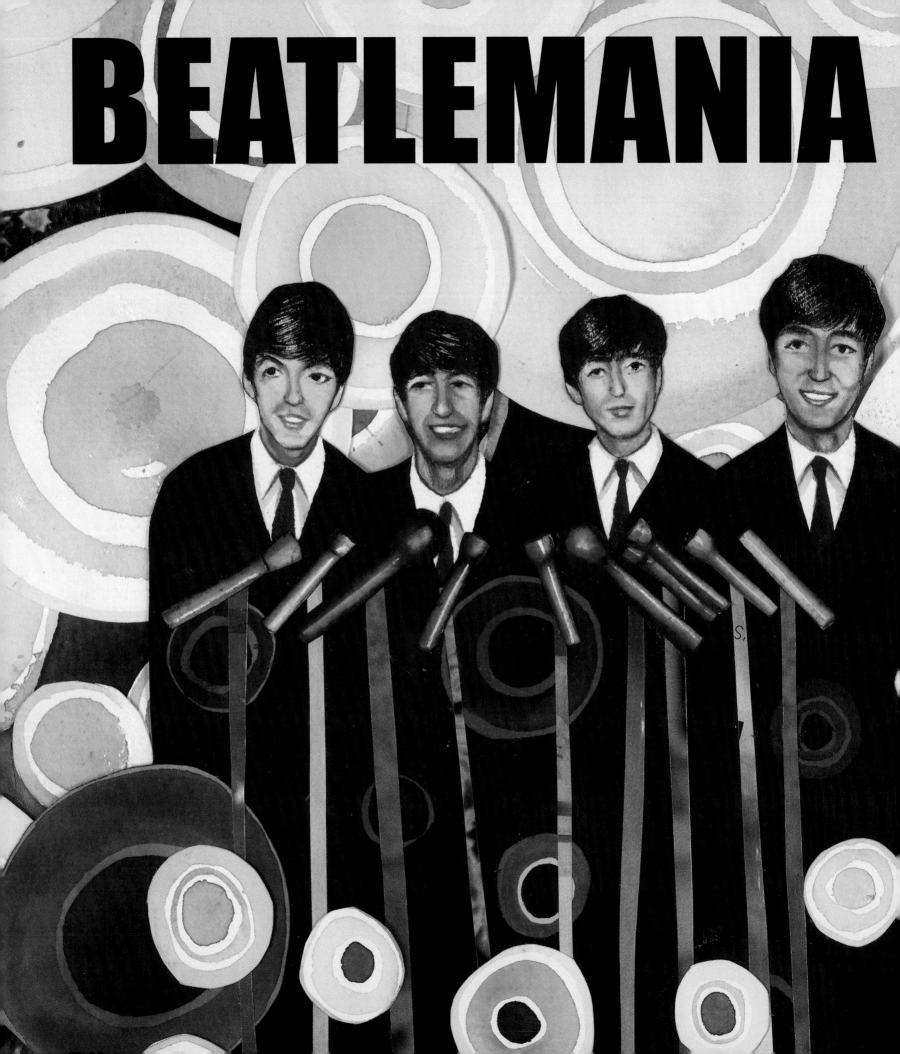

swept the world!

Wherever the Beatles went,
flashbulbs popped,
reporters shouted questions,
fans screamed and shrieked
and fought with police
to get close enough to touch them.

Wherever they performed,
before John sang his first word,
the screaming was so loud,
he couldn't hear George
or Paul or Ringo play.
And the fans couldn't
hear them either.

Say you're looking
for a place to go
Where Nobody knows
your name . . .
with one Eye on
the Hall of Fame

Help me if yo

And I do

Help me ge

Won't you please

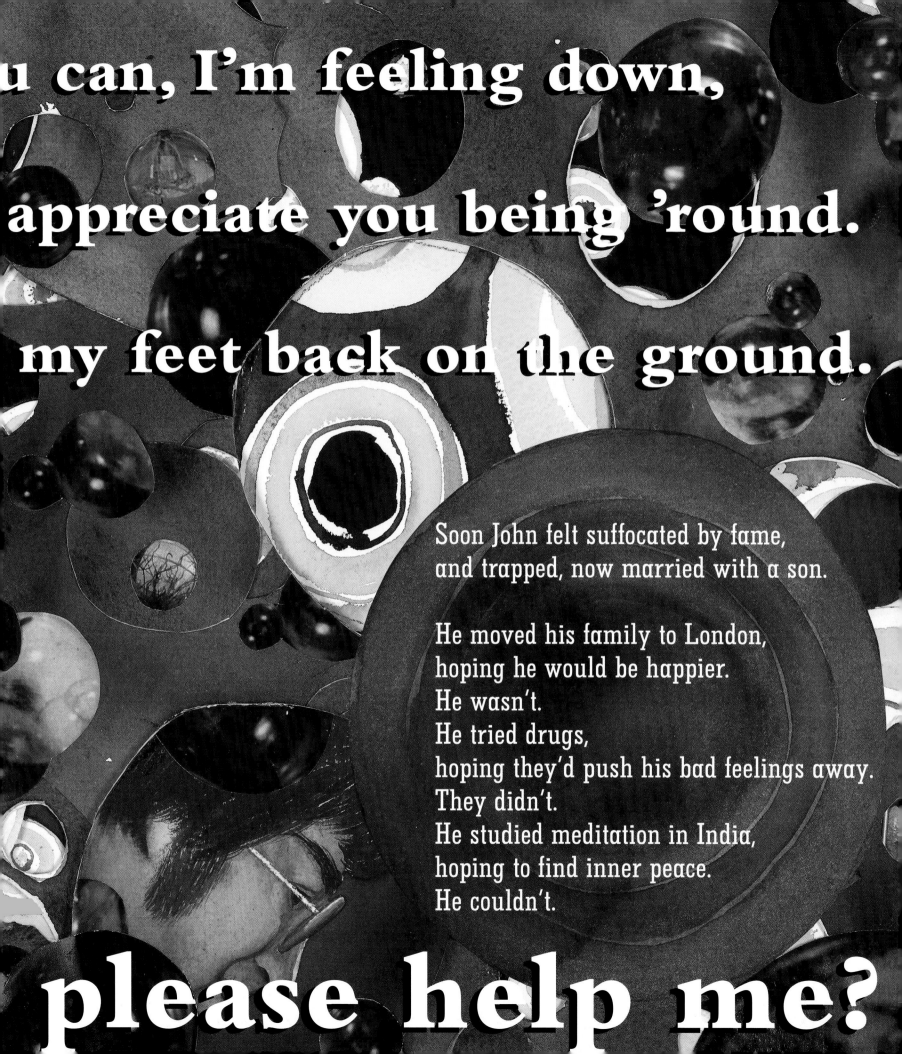

u can, I'm feeling down,

appreciate you being 'round.

my feet back on the ground.

Soon John felt suffocated by fame,
and trapped, now married with a son.

He moved his family to London,
hoping he would be happier.
He wasn't.
He tried drugs,
hoping they'd push his bad feelings away.
They didn't.
He studied meditation in India,
hoping to find inner peace.
He couldn't.

please help me?

People in London were buzzing
about an artist named Yoko Ono.
John went to see her new show.

Yoko handed John a card.
Breathe, read the card.
He did, and laughed silently.

A magnifying glass was hanging
from a painting on the ceiling.
He looked through it
and read *Yes* in tiny letters.
How wonderful to see *Yes* instead of *No*.

yes is the answer
and you know that
for sure.
yes is surrender
you gotta let it,
you gotta let it go

The Beatles stopped touring
and wrote new songs.

People felt longing in John's song
about his childhood haunt.

Let me take you down
'cause I'm going to
Strawberry Fields.
Nothing is real

People laughed at his nonsense

His son Julian painted a picture.
John responded with a song.

Some people called John a poet.

Picture yourself
in a boat on a river

with tangerine trees and
marmalade skies.

Somebody calls you,
you answer quite slowly,

a girl with
kaleidoscope
eyes.

In a recording studio,
the Beatles experimented with sounds
never before heard in rock music.

Woke up got out of bed

Let an alarm clock ring.
Blow bubbles through a straw.

Dragged a comb across my head

Swirl water in a bucket.
Play a comb!

Found my way down stairs and

Add organs, sitars, mellotrons.
Have forty musicians play their
lowest notes to their highest
as fast or slow as they want.
Play the melody forward, then backward.

And somebody spoke and I went

Rock 'n' roll—anything you wanted it to be.
Popular music was changed forever.

drank a cup . . .

into a dream

Despite the praise,
John secretly wanted to leave the group.
But he was scared.

I don't believe
in Beatles.
I just believe in me.
Yoko and me.
And that's reality.

He believed Yoko Ono could help him
with the "blank spaces" ahead.
He divorced his wife and married Yoko.

All my little plans
    and schemes
Lost in some
    forgotten dream
Seems that all I was
    really doing
Was waiting for you

War raged in Vietnam.
John and Yoko wanted to end violence.
They held a "bed-in" for peace
as a honeymoon.

John dreamed of writing a song
as powerful as "We Shall Overcome,"
the anthem of the civil rights movement.
One day, the lyrics came to him:

All we are saying is give peace a chance.

Soon, wherever people protested war,
they sang John's song.

John was not the only Beatle who was unhappy.

After ten years of working together,
John, Paul, George, and Ringo
went their separate ways.

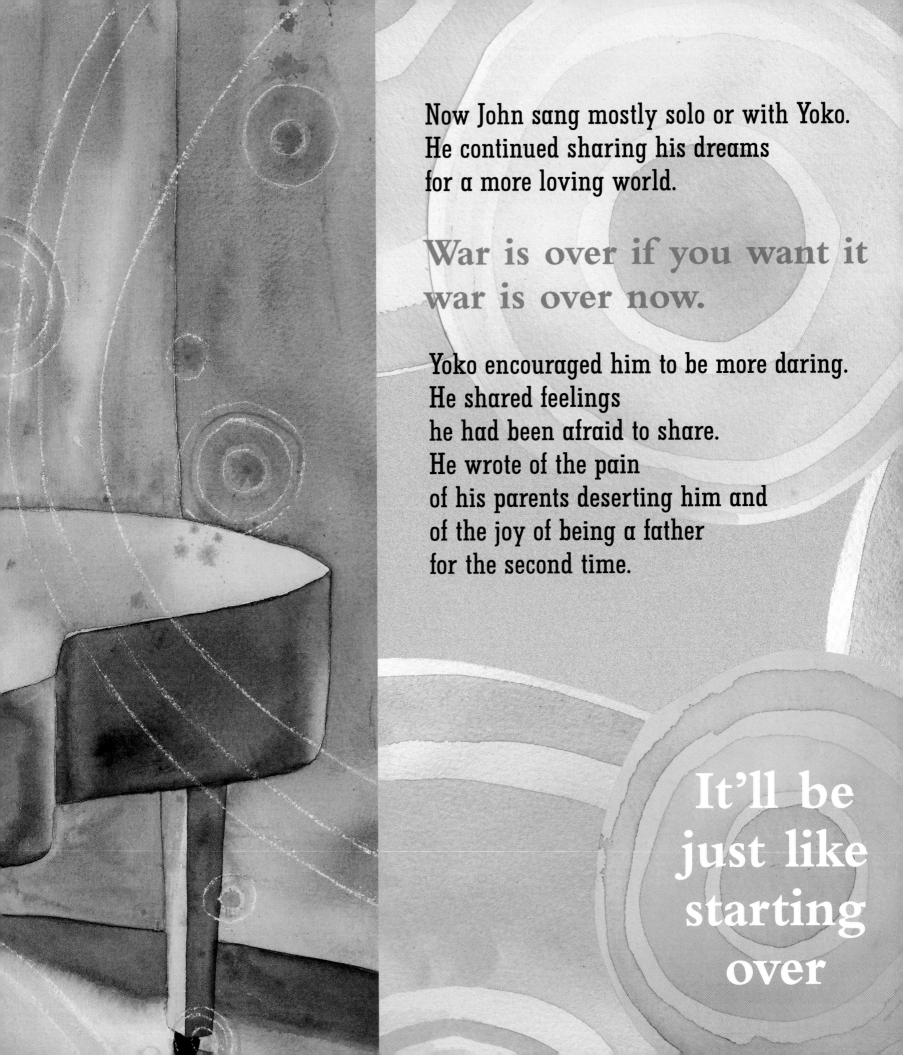

Now John sang mostly solo or with Yoko.
He continued sharing his dreams
for a more loving world.

War is over if you want it
war is over now.

Yoko encouraged him to be more daring.
He shared feelings
he had been afraid to share.
He wrote of the pain
of his parents deserting him and
of the joy of being a father
for the second time.

It'll be
just like
starting
over

He dreamed about being
sixty and being with Yoko.

Grow old along with me
The best is yet to be
When our time has come
We will be as one

That dream did not come true.

John Lennon was murdered when
he was only forty years old.

Now it's up to us to make John's dream
for the world come true. . . .

Imagine all the
living life in pe
You may say I'
But I'm not th
I hope some da
And the world

people

ace,

m a dreamer,

e only one.

y you'll join us

will live as one.

IMPORTANT DATES

- **October 9, 1940**: John Winston Lennon is born in Liverpool, England, to Julia and Alfred Lennon.
- **1945**: John goes to live with Mimi and George Smith.
- **July 6, 1957**: John asks Paul McCartney to join the Quarrymen.
- **September 1957**: John enters Liverpool Art College.
- **1958**: George Harrison joins the Quarrymen.
- **July 15, 1958**: John's mother dies in a car accident.
- **1960**: John names the group the "Beatles."
- **August 1962**: The record company EMI signs the Beatles. Ringo Starr replaces their drummer, Pete Best.
- **August 23, 1962**: John marries Cynthia Powell.
- **October 1962**: "Love Me Do" single is #21 on British charts.
- **April 8, 1963**: Julian Lennon is born.
- **May 1963**: The album *Please, Please Me* holds #1 spot for thirty weeks in England.
- **November 1963**: Beatlemania hits Britain.
- **November 1963**: The album *With the Beatles* is #1 for twenty-two weeks in England.
- **February 9, 1964**: Seventy-three million people watch the Beatles perform on *The Ed Sullivan Show*.
- **March 1964**: John Lennon's *In His Own Write* is published.
- **Summer 1964**: The Beatles tour the United States.
- **November 9, 1966**: John meets Yoko Ono.
- **Spring 1968**: The Beatles leave for India.
- **January 30, 1969**: The Beatles perform live for the last time on the roof of the headquarters of Apple Records in London, England.
- **March 20, 1969**: John and Yoko marry.
- **March 25–31, 1969**: Bed-in for Peace event takes place in the Amsterdam Hilton Hotel, Holland.
- **May 26, 1969**: At a second bed-in, in Montreal, John writes "Give Peace a Chance."
- **1970**: The Beatles pursue individual careers. John forms Plastic Ono Band with Yoko on vocals.
- **August 1971**: John and Yoko move to New York City.
- **October 9, 1975**: Sean Ono Lennon is born in New York City.
- **December 8, 1980**: John Lennon dies.

SELECTED DISCOGRAPHY

Beatles Albums

Please, Please Me. EMI Records, 1963.

Meet the Beatles. Capitol Records, January 1964.

A Hard Day's Night (Original Sound Track Album). Capitol Records, 1964.

Help! (Original Sound Track Album). Capitol Records, 1965.

Rubber Soul. Capitol Records, 1965.

Revolver. Capitol Records, 1966.

Sgt. Pepper's Lonely Hearts Club Band. Capitol Records, 1967.

Magical Mystery Tour. Capitol Records, 1967.

The White Album. Apple Records, 1968.

Yellow Submarine. Apple Records, 1969.

Abbey Road. Apple Records, 1969.

Let It Be (Original Sound Track Album). Apple Records, 1970.

Solo Albums and Albums with Yoko Ono

Two Virgins. Apple Records, 1968. (John and Yoko Ono)

Life With the Lions. Apple Records, 1969. (John and Yoko Ono)

Wedding Album. Apple Records, 1969. (John and Yoko Ono)

Live Peace in Toronto. Apple Records, 1969. (Plastic Ono Band)

John Lennon/Plastic Ono Band. Apple Records, 1970.

Imagine. Apple Records, 1971.

Mind Games. Apple Records, 1973.

Walls and Bridges. Apple Records, 1974.

Rock'n'Roll. Apple Records, 1975.

Double Fantasy. Geffen Records, 1980. (John and Yoko Ono)

Milk and Honey. Polydor, 1984. (John and Yoko Ono)

SELECTED RESEARCH SOURCES

Beatles. *The Beatles Anthology.* San Francisco: Chronicle Books, LLC, 2000.

Brown, Charles T. *The Art of Rock and Roll.* Englewood Cliffs, N.J.: Prentice Hall, Inc., 1963.

Du Noyer, Paul. *John Lennon: Whatever Gets You Through the Night.* New York: Thunder's Mouth Press, 1999.

Giuliano, Geoffrey. *Lennon in America.* New York: Cooper Square Press, 2000.

Giuliano, Geoffrey, and Brenda Giuliano. *The Lost Lennon Interviews.* Holbrook, Mass.: Adams Media Corporation, 1996.

Goldman, Albert. *The Lives of John Lennon.* New York: William Morrow and Company, 1988.

Hieronimus, Dr. Robert R. *Inside the Yellow Submarine: The Making of the Beatles' Animated Classic.* Iola, Wisc.: Krause Publications, 2002.

Imagine: The Definitive Film Portrait. VHS. Warner Studios, 1998.

Knight, Judson. *Abbey Road to Zapple Records: A Beatles Encyclopedia.* Dallas: Taylor Publishing Company, 1999.

Lennon, John. *Skywriting by Word of Mouth: And Other Writings, Including the Ballad of John & Yoko.* New York: HarperCollins, 1996.

Mahoney, J. W. "Transmodern Yoko." *Art in America,* February 2002.

Mellers, Wilfrid. *Twilight of the Gods: The Music of the Beatles.* New York: Macmillan Library Reference, 1975.

Turner, Steve. *A Hard Day's Write: The Story Behind Every Beatles Song.* New York: HarperCollins, 1999.

Weiner, Jon. *Come Together: John Lennon in His Time.* Chicago: University of Illinois Press, 1990.

Wenner, Jann S. *Lennon Remembers.* New York: Verso, 2000.

If you want to learn more about the people and music in this book, read:

Corbin, Carole Lynn. *John Lennon.* Chicago, Franklin Watts, 1982.

George-Warren, Holly. *Shake, Rattle and Roll: The Founders of Rock and Roll.* Boston: Houghton Mifflin, 2001.

Glassman, Bruce S. *John Lennon and Paul McCartney: Their Magic and Their Music.* Farmington Hills, Mich.: Gale Group, 1995.

Gogerly, Liz. *John Lennon: Voice of a Generation.* Chicago: Raintree Publishing, 2002.

Leigh, Vanora. *John Lennon.* Chicago: Franklin Watts, 1986.

Lennon, John. Adapted by Al Naclerio. *Real Love: The Drawings for Sean.* New York: Random House Children's Books, 1999.

Littlesugar, Amy. *Shake Rag: From the Life of Elvis Presley.* Penguin Putnam Books for Young Readers, 2001.

Stockdale, Tom. *John Lennon.* Broomall, Penn.: Chelsea House Publishing, 1997.

Venezia, Mike. *The Beatles.* New York: Scholastic Library Publishing, 1997.

Wootton, Richard. *John Lennon.* New York: Random House Books for Young Readers. 1985.

Web Sites:

The Internet has thousands of sites on John Lennon, the Beatles, and others in the history of rock and roll. Many of these are not official Web sites. Use caution, for information and lyrics may be inaccurate.

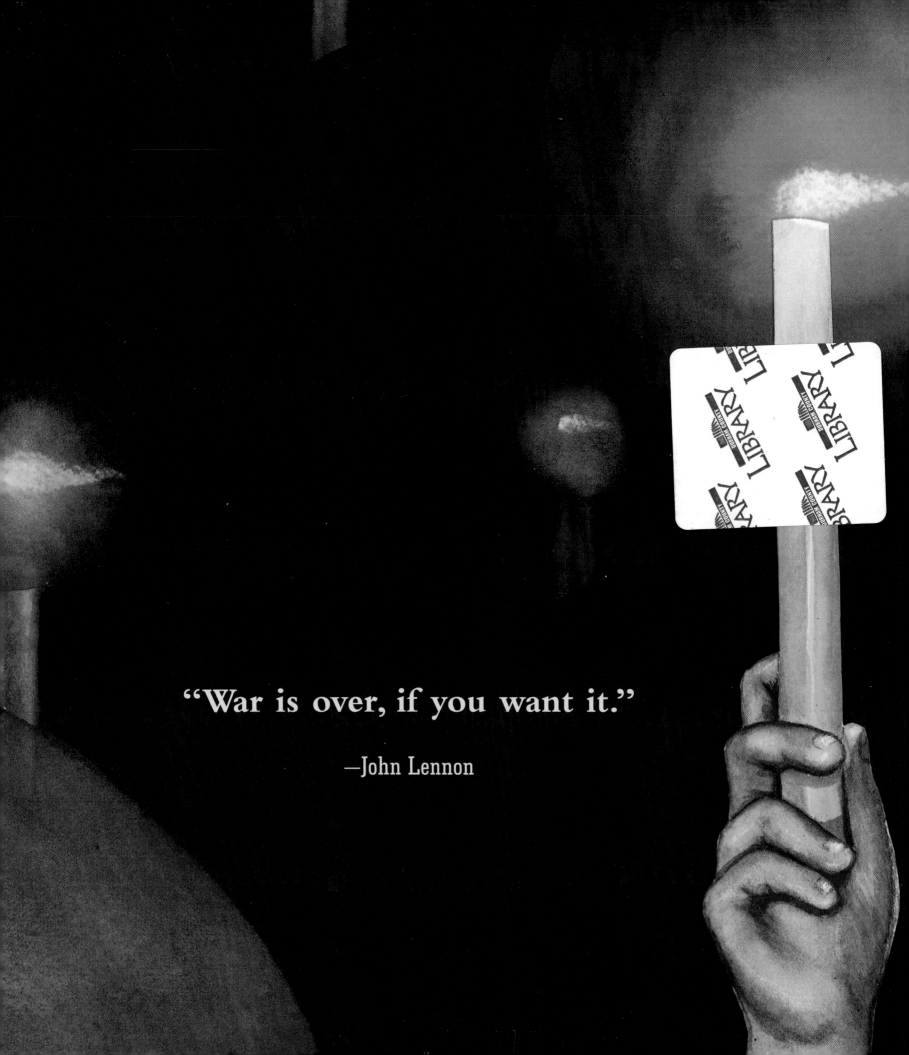

"War is over, if you want it."

—John Lennon